Hacking Portugal

Making Portugal a global player in
Software Development

Dinis Cruz

Hacking Portugal

Making Portugal a global player in Software Development

Dinis Cruz

ISBN 978-1540743633

Leanpub

This is a Leanpub book. Leanpub empowers authors and publishers with the Lean Publishing process. Lean Publishing is the act of publishing an in-progress ebook using lightweight tools and many iterations to get reader feedback, pivot until you have the right book and build traction once you do.

Also By Dinis Cruz

Practical Git and GitHub

Practical AngularJS

Practical Eclipse Plugin Development

Practical Jni4Net

Thoughts on OWASP

Exploiting MVC Model Binding

Practical O2 Platform Tools

SecDevOps Risk Workflow

Contents

CONTENTS

Introduction

This book is based, and expands, on a presentation given at BSidesLisbon on 9 November 2016.

The ideas I consider here look to the future, as some of the concepts are too radical until the AppSec problem becomes much bigger. They are ideas for a future when solutions are wanted.

As technology and software become more and more important to Portuguese society, it is time for Portugal to take them more seriously, and become a real player in that world. This book discusses several ideas to make Portugal a place where programming, TDD, Open Source, learning how to code, hacking (aka bug-bounty style), and DevOps receive the consideration, investment and respect that they deserve. Application Security can act as an enabler for this transformation, due to its focus on how code and apps work, and its enormous advances in secure-coding, testing, dev-ops and quality.

Why I'm doing this

I have been studying this area, and its various challenges and possibilities, for some time, and for many reasons.

The current economic model is not working for secure code and secure software development, and it is not working for many parts of the general population. In many cases, it doesn't make business sense to spend the time and effort creating secure code, because the customer cannot measure it. I believe we must innovate our way out of this problem.

I have considerable experience working in the AppSec industry, and this allows me to see the problems coming down the line. However, the same experience also allows me to see solutions to the problems, and I want to share and discuss my ideas for these solutions. Moreover, I want to create a safe future for our kids.

Summary of Chapters

In 'Portuguese network to be hostile to insecure code', I discuss the possibility of Portugal becoming a hostile place to create, publish or host insecure apps or IoT appliances. The creation of a safe internet in Portugal is possible, but it will need the support and input of Creative Commons, regulatory and market forces, and communities, for it to work. We need new ideas and different perspectives for this to succeed.

'Hackers' considers the term 'hackers', as opposed to 'attackers', and discusses how hacking can help to create a secure internet for Portugal. The sound ethical values of the hacking community can inspire the next generation of internet users.

'How Secure is Portugal' examines how Portugal, despite being a digital country with a great dependence on software, has many vulnerabilities and exploitable assets, which make it highly vulnerable to cyber-attack in the future. Implementing the correct measures, for example by utilizing and increasing the InfoSec and AppSec talent available in Portugal, will help to mitigate the risk of attack.

'Portuguese Hacking Service' suggests that 15-20 year olds should undertake their 'Hacking Service', a new version of the former Portuguese Military Service. The chapter also looks at the Portuguese military budget, and argues that a percentage of it should be diverted into virtual battles against cyber-attacks on Portuguese assets. Everyone should learn to hack, including criminals and retired people, for the general benefit of Portuguese Government, business, and society. New structures like a 'Portuguese Hackathon League' would develop Portugal into a country as famous for hacking as it is for football.

'Portuguese Innovations' looks to the glorious history of Portuguese innovation, from the Carrack ship to marmalade, to the more recent success of drugs decriminalization in Portugal, which has dramatically reduced the rate of drugs overdoses and drug-related deaths.

'Leader in cyber and application security' looks to the future of Portuguese innovation, and notes that where Portugal led the way in maritime navigation and innovation in the past, it should now become a world leader in coding and AppSec. The chapter offers some pointers to developers. It also describes cyber security as a public health problem, and states that the techniques used to train cyber security specialists should resemble those used to train medical professionals.

'Privacy' discusses the importance of privacy to the individual. It notes how cryptography can help the individual to control their data, in a world where some governments and businesses act to reduce, or remove, the technological privacy of the citizen.

The chapter goes on to consider the need for disclosure in companies, and the role whistleblowers have to encourage disclosure and improve how markets work. We need legislation that protects whistleblowers and compels disclosure, to create an environment where there is maximum privacy for the individual, and maximum transparency for companies. The way the music industry resisted technological innovation is used as an example of the negative consequences of secrecy and non-disclosure.

'Open Source' develops the ideas discussed in 'Privacy', and notes the importance of openness and transparency to the success of the arguments presented. Programs such as OWASP, Git, and FOSS can help to achieve the desired level of transparency. The chapter discusses the need for Open Source to become a *lingua franca*, and it suggests specific legislative changes to increase transparency at government and corporate level.

'Government' acknowledges the role of government as a benign influence to effect change. The chapter recommends the establishment of a Ministry of Code and a Software Testing Institute, but warns that these must be matched by sensible regulation and governance. It also proposes a Clear Software Act, focused on code quality and security. Bug bounties are suggested, and the role of the insurance industry discussed. The European Union, and the creation of new currencies for weaker economies, are also treated.

'Why Portugal' explains why, from its size to its culture and economy, Portugal is the best location to implement the ideas presented in this book. The chapter concludes with the options facing Portugal: to become a holiday destination, or a Powerhouse of Technology, ready to lead the world in code and security.

'Actions and Recommendations' summarises the actions and recommendations suggested throughout the book.

Acknowledgements

Thanks to BSidesLisbon for the opportunity to deliver the Keynote in 2017, Ann Marie for amazing edits, Paulo Coimbra for all late night discussions, and many others that helped me consolidate these ideas.

Please give me your feedback

This is the first version of this book and I'm planning in making frequent updates.

All content is hosted at the Book_Hacking_Portugal[1] GitHub site, where you also will find a location to enter issues and questions[2].

You can also email me directly at dinis.cruz@owasp.org

Feedback is highly appreciated, so let me know what you think of the ideas presented in this book :)

---

[1]https://github.com/DinisCruz/Book_Hacking_Portugal
[2]https://github.com/DinisCruz/Book_Hacking_Portugal/issues

Portugal should be hostile to insecure code

Here is the key concept of this book:

"Make Portugal's internet a hostile place to create, publish, and host insecure applications and IoT appliances"

I want the Portuguese internet to be safe. To achieve this, we will need strong Collaborative Commons and community support. We will also need strong enforcement, regulation, and market pressure to make this happen.

Portugal has sovereignty over its network, and can pass laws to protect it.

I want bots that scan the Portuguese internet to attack, and destroy (in a nice way), insecure code and insecure applications running inside its cyber space.

We need health-services for code, with home visits to software developers and other companies to help them improve how they handle their IT infrastructure.

This is not about making everyone in Portugal into highly technical computer experts.

We want to create an elite section of professionals that are 'best in class', who can make the internet, and coding, safe for everybody.

Blaming the users for clicking on the wrong link, or blaming developers for using the 'wrong library', confuses the cause of the problem with its side effects.

A key objective is to make security and AppSec invisible.

Security and AppSec are there to protect and ensure that insecure code is detected and mitigated. This is not achieved by using command and control, but rather with decentralization, transparency, ownership and trust.

The cost of bugs and bad, or insecure, software is already significant, even for a country the size of Portugal.

Attack vulnerable code

I want vulnerable apps and appliances that are plugged into the Portuguese national network to be hacked within seconds.

These apps and appliances should be hacked by 'good guys', who are trying to help by fixing, or by disabling, as necessary.

Government should have a mandate to authorize hacking to vulnerable devices (computers, routes, IoT) and fix them. In a way, this mandate is also 'given' by the manufacturer once they push apps/code that contain vulnerabilities.

Insurance companies should support this initiative, especially for cases where something goes wrong and a device is 'bricked'.

Next generation of internet users

I don't want the next generation of users to fear the internet, or to allow such a fear to govern their actions.

I don't want them to first experience the internet in a negative way, where one of their possessions, such as a doll, a light bulb, a website, an email account, a car, or even a door (where they are asked to pay ransomware), has been hacked.

PHS - Portuguese Hacking Service

In the past Portugal had a Military Service called 'Servico Militar Obrigatorio'. We should update this service to the 21st Century and make it a Hacking Service for 15 to 21 year olds, with the following mission objectives:

- hack everything that is plugged-in to Portugal's network
- hack companies with public bug-bounties
- code-review Open Source code developed in Portugal
- code-review code marked as 'strategic interest for Portugal' (i.e. widely used by Portuguese companies and mission critical for them)
- contribute to Open Source projects with patches and fixes
- help SMEs with their digital security and DevOps

Portuguese hackathon league

In the same way that we have a national football league, Portugal should organize and host regular Hackathons[3], as part of a new, national, hackathon league.

The Portuguese hacking teams should go to DefCon, and they should be sponsored by Portuguese government and business. These teams should be a source of national pride.

The best way to learn is to solve a problem from a variety of angles, using a variety of technologies.

Other sources of talent

Everyone should learn to hack, including children, professionals who want to change their careers, and unemployed people. These

---

[3]https://en.wikipedia.org/wiki/Hackathon

great sources of talent should be utilized for the benefit of Portugal. Two groups that should also be taught to hack are convicted criminals and retired people.

Convicted criminals

Teaching convicted criminals to hack would make good use of their skills. It would give them an alternative career to crime, and it would show them a way to make money legally. They would learn a more ethical approach to work, and they would learn the value of collaborating.

Most criminals who find themselves in prison do so from bad choices or unfortunate events, and many of them deserve a chance at a better life.

Retired people

We lose a lot by not using the expertise of retired people, and by not learning from them. In the past, older people were the wise ones, and respected for their knowledge and experience. They are engineers, doctors, programmers, teachers, accountants, architects, parents, etc. People grow old, not because of age, but because they stop being mentally and physically active.

Working together

In the world of technology or hacking, it is okay to have teams made up of representatives from the following groups:

- 16 year olds
- graduates
- retired people
- convicted criminals

- a dog[4]
- a professional

If they are capable, can work together, respect each other, and deliver on their tasks, they will succeed.

---

[4]https://en.wikipedia.org/wiki/On_the_Internet,_nobody_knows_you%27re_a_dog

"Made in Portugal"

Best in world

Portugal has one of the best football teams in the world.

Portugal is currently 8th in the Fifa world ranking[5]

Just as in football, Portugal needs to be one of the best in the world in Coding and Cyber/App Security.

Portugal as a leader in AppSec

Portugal could be a leader in AppSec. Portugal has a rich history of providing leading innovators and ground-breaking researchers in navigation, in maritime research, and exploration. Portugal must build on its history of innovation and achievement, and become a world leader in coding.

Portuguese researchers are highly innovative. They are following this great history of leading important change and discovery.

"Code Made in Portugal" brand

Code that is "Made in Portugal" is the key for the Portuguese economy, and for Europe's sustainability. It will have a huge influence, and it will be essential to create supply chains of quality and talent.

Good software development teams (from developers to management) are one of the most important assets of a company and country. They are the ones who add value. They create reality, and ultimately, they control your lives.

---

[5]http://www.fifa.com/fifa-world-ranking/associations/association=por/men/index.html

"Made in Portugal" will encourage and foment the PT software industry, and this will in turn have a multiplier effect in other industries.

The Age of Sustainability is upon us, and Portugal should be at its centre.

Past innovations

Portugal has a great history of inventions:

- Carrack (Nau) - the Oceanic Carrack (a new and different model, and the largest carrack of its time)
- Galleon (the Oceanic Galleon)
- Square-rigged caravel (Round caravel)
- The Nonius
- The Mariner's astrolabe
- The Passarola, the first known airship
- The Pyreliophorus
- Tempura

Drugs Decriminalization

The decriminalization of drugs in Portugal is a great success story of what happens when bold decisions are made. In 14 years, Portugal went from a very high rate[6] of consumption and overdose, to one of the lowest.

Portuguese innovation for the 21st Century

The investment and focus I propose in these pages are what 21st century infrastructure is all about. At the moment, Portugal lacks the DataCenters, and the big data pipes that will attract companies to host their sites in Portugal. The development of Portugal as a safe, fast, and well-maintained data hub will make sure this investment and growth happens.

Portugal is missing from the current AWS global infrastructure.

---

[6]https://mic.com/articles/120403/14-years-after-decriminalizing-drugs-one-chart-shows-why-portugal-s-experiment-has-worked

Portugal is a great place to organize global conferences (Web Summit 2016, OWASP Summits 2011), since it is literally in the middle of the world. We need to make Portugal as attractive a location for writing, hosting and deploying code (i.e. applications).

Tesla in Portugal

A major objective for Portugal is to be so attractive to companies that they locate in Portugal. The Portuguese government and its agencies should aim to attract Tesla to have factories and R&D facilities in Portugal. This shouldn't be negotiated as a 'favour' or via 'soft bribes'. It should happen because Portugal has the people, processes, and technology to fulfil Tesla's vision.

There are great synergies between Tesla's 'SolarCity' and the current investment and capabilities of solar power in Portugal, which is a great success story, as Portugal is already producing quite a lot of its electricity using alternative energies.

PT needs to develop the equivalent of the Tesla Gigafactories to be energy interdependent.

How Secure is Portugal?

How secure and safe are Portuguese companies and infrastructures?

Portugal today is a very digital country, and most Portuguese companies are software companies. If you look at how they operate, they all use software and are controlled by software.

The question is, how secure are they? How safe are they? By 'secure', I mean how well can they sustain an attack? How well can they detect and react to a possible attack on their digital infrastructure? What is the probability of an attack happening in the short term?

Our security model is based on lack of attackers

Portugal is safe because there are not enough attackers targeting the current insecurities of the system. This will probably remain the case for the next couple of years. The problem is what happens after that, when the criminals improve their business models and start to focus on Portuguese assets.

The bottom line is that the current 'secure state' of Portugal's government, companies, & people, where the likelihood of an attack happening is low, depends on the following assumptions:

- A low number of attackers
- A low level of skill among existing attackers
- The existing attackers' unsophisticated business model

So, although these are contradictory concepts, my thesis is that Portugal is both highly insecure, and, for the moment, quite safe.

The Emperor's new clothes

Portuguese government agencies and companies say they **are secure**. This is not true. They are NOT secure, and have many high-risk vulnerabilities and exploitable assets. It is very important that we accept this fact so that we can find the necessary political, economic, educational, and social solutions. For now, "The Emperor has no clothes".

There are no silver bullets or easy solutions, and anyone who says so is a snake-oil merchant.

The ideas in this book are about making Portugal a player, rather than being played, and giving Portugal a chance to defend itself, and improve Portuguese society. The worst aspect of our status is that we are not prepared for what is coming next, in terms of cyber crime and Application Security.

Our response to terrorist incidents in the past shows how badly we can respond as a society to security incidents for which we are not prepared.

Think I'm wrong?

If you don't believe that Portugal is insecure, then prove me wrong in your answers to the following questions: * Where is the evidence of Security and AppSec practices? * How big is the Cyber/App Security market in Portugal? * How many threat models are created per week? * How many lines of code are reviewed for security per week (aka 'security eyeballs')? (Bear in mind that secure code reviews are very different from normal code reviews).

The current Portuguese security model is based on *"Security Fairies' magic pixie dust"*. However, the good news is that we have lots of great InfoSec and AppSec talent in Portugal.

The financial markets hack

I would argue that Portugal has already been a victim of certain kinds of financial manipulation. If you look at what happened during the financial crisis, a substantial part of it was artificially created by the markets.

The markets pushed the Portuguese economy hard and made a lot of money by betting that Portugal was going to struggle, and would continue to struggle, in the financial markets.

Thank your attackers

"If the attacker tells you about the attack, they are your friends".

The real attackers (namely criminals and nation states) will not tell you since it is against their own interests to do so. Once you know about the attack, you will find a way to protect and fix the relevant vulnerability.

The positive side effects of any public attack (data dumps, site defacing, DDoS) are bigger budgets, board-level attention and demands for security, an increase in AppSec staff hires, and more collaboration between 'companies on the defense side of things'.

Military

It is probably fair to say that Portuguese cyber and code defences are as good as Portugal's current military status (see Portuguese Armed Forces[7] and Portuguese Air Force[8]).

The problem is that the cyber attackers who will hit Portugal are as sophisticated as the best soldiers, and armies.

Imagine the Portuguese army against the UK, France or Russia, not to mention the US or China.

---

[7]https://en.wikipedia.org/wiki/Portuguese_Armed_Forces
[8]https://en.wikipedia.org/wiki/Portuguese_Air_Force

Note how even the best companies and security agencies in the world are not able to detect and mitigate most attacks, as evidenced by recent DDoS attacks and zero-days exploits. The following video gives a humorous idea of what a DDoS attack feels like[9]

Why do we have F16s?

Why does Portugal need an offensive air force? I understand the need to have a civil air-force, to combat fires or for border patrols, but an offensive air force, with F16s? What is the 'war scenario' where that makes sense?

The way you fight an airborne battle in the 21st century is by hacking into the offensive planes/drones via their communication channels. The novel Ghost Fleet[10] (Singer & Cole, 2015) imagines the next, virtual, world war.

The military budget for Portugal in 2014 was just over 2.1 Billion Euros[11]. I would argue that the government should allocate 10% of the current military budget to fund investment in cyber/app security, and the huge skills shortage in this area.

Hit by the crossfire

The important question is *"Do we want to do something about this, or be hit by the cross-fire?"* If we do not consider this question, and address the huge skills shortage in cyber/app security that exists in Portugal, we will pay a heavy price.

As attackers become more sophisticated, they will gravitate to countries and companies with weaker defenses, since these take longer to ramp up their security when an attack occurs.

---

[9]https://twitter.com/macbroadcast/status/791837377186725888
[10]https://www.amazon.co.uk/Ghost-Fleet-Novel-Next-World/dp/0544142845
[11]https://en.wikipedia.org/wiki/Portuguese_Armed_Forces

Public health analogy

Red or blue pill?

We need to choose whether the paradigm for cyber security is one based on the military (offensive, top-down) or on public health (defensive, distributed).

There is a reason why the army is not supposed to be involved in civil activities such as crowd control or disaster support. The military is there to defend us from our enemies. It is the police and other civil forces who focus on protecting the individual. The military and the police have very different perspectives. One must always assume that other side is 'guilty until proven innocent, and it could be attacking me', and the other must always assume that the other side is 'innocent until proven guilty, and my job is to protect him/her'.

Public health problem

Cyber Security is a public health problem.

To address the problem, we should train cyber/AppSec specialists using similar techniques to the ones we use to train doctors, nurses, and other medical professionals.

We have an epidemic at hand, and we need to gain immunity.

The decisions that we make in the next couple of years will determine how well prepared we will be to deal with wider outbreaks, and how quickly we can learn.

Sane defense model

Our defense model should not be based on having no vulnerabilities, no insecure code, no malicious developers, no compromised APs/dependencies, no zero-days issues.

Our defense model should be based on the attacker making mistakes, and our being ready to detect and mitigate their actions.

Stuxnet was caught via a mistake that caused a crash in an obscure anti-virus product (see Zetter, K. (2015) Countdown to Zero Day[12]).

The Portuguese National Cyber Security Strategy[13] is a good document with good ideas and action plans, but it does not mention secure coding or addressing the root causes of the problems. We tend to confuse the symptoms with the causes.

Where is the AppSec industry?

The AppSec industry in Portugal is comparatively small. There are very few Portuguese companies with public AppSec teams. The market for security companies is small, and while there are a couple of interesting pen testing companies, you don't see a lot of activity in that space.

The creation of an AppSec infrastructure is a direct consequence of being attacked. After an attack, companies create AppSec teams and hire security experts. If anything, Portugal exports its security experts. I know many great Portuguese AppSec and InfoSec specialists in the UK.

The problem is, security experts aren't being recruited to Portugal. At the moment, countries like the UK, that are more evolved in AppSec, are recruiting, but Portugal should also be hiring AppSec talent.

Be proactive

The reality is the Portuguese AppSec industry isn't very mature. The question is, does Portugal want to be like the rest of Europe and get

---

[12]https://www.amazon.com/Countdown-Zero-Day-Stuxnet-Digital/dp/0770436196

[13]https://www.enisa.europa.eu/topics/national-cyber-security-strategies/ncss-map/portuguese-national-cyber-security-strategy/view

caught in the crossfire? Or does it want to be proactive, and create an industry which could become very powerful, very effective, and very profitable for Portugal, and could also help to secure Europe and help the world?

Hack like football

Why is Portugal so good at football?

Portugal is good at football for many reasons. Almost everyone can play football, and our kids play it all the time. When they play, and give the game their full concentration, they are in "the zone", which is the optimal place for them to learn. School sports activities also encourage and support football.

Football offers good social rewards and helps to build communities. Local clubs provide a great support system in the way they find, select, and nurture talent.

Finally, the prospect of good financial rewards for many players, and not just at national and international level, also encourages an interest in, and support for, the game.

Let's do the same for hacking

Everybody can learn to hack, from kids to the unemployed, to convicted criminals, to retired people. Our kids should be hacking all the time. Many of them will love learning to hack, so they will be "in the zone" when they do. Schools can support these activities, and individual schools' prowess at hacking should become a source of pride. A support network can find, select, and nurture hacking talent, and there will be good financial rewards for hackers, as there is a chronic shortage of skills in this industry.

Hacking

Hacking created the Internet

It is important to state that hackers are the good guys.

To 'Hack' is to solve problems, to find innovative solutions in a creative way.

The press abuses the term 'hacker'. Instead, they should qualify the word by saying 'Malicious Hackers' or 'Cyber Attackers' or 'Cyber Criminals'.

The internet and most of the technology we use today was dreamed of, and created by, hackers.

Hackers' values

The software, InfoSec and hacking community has a strong ethical foundation, based on the following qualities:

- sharing
- respect
- friendship
- trust
- non-discrimination
- humanity and companionship

We want to inspire the next generation with these values. To do this, we need to provide an alternative narrative to the current mainstream narrative of 'lies', 'non-experts-welcome' and 'info-tainment'.

Our alternative benefits from the following strong qualities:

- business/commercial understanding

- money-generation capabilities (outside of the 'proprietary and lock-in' business models)
- understanding that profit is good and healthy

Creating Your future

The hackers who grow-up creating distributed bots to attack insecure apps/code/appliance in the Portuguese network (as part of the Portuguese Hacking Service) are the same ones who will create a 'distributed peer-to-peer drone network, to combat fires in Portugal'.

Be different

If 99.9% of the world doesn't agree with your ideas, this doesn't mean you shouldn't pursue them. Most things you value (and do) today were once illegal and considered immoral.

(Add image of barefoot running)

Open Source

Openness is key

For most of the ideas defended here to work, and not back-fire, even if they create strong command-and-control systems/environments, we need a very high degree of transparency and openness. This is exactly what the Open Source and Creative Commons worlds provide.

OWASP is a good example of an organization that has a very strong open model it applies to everything, right through to its governance and fiscal transparency.

Git is also a key part of this, since Git enables effective collaboration, allowing others to contribute, even if they are direct competitors in other products or services.

FOSS Values

FOSS (Free and Open Source) programs are a good model to use, as they allow users to share and collaborate programs. They can empower users, and could potentially create thousands of Portugal-based FOSS companies.

Portugal should embrace organizations like OWASP, which has held two summits in Portugal (Add pics and logos).

The positive values of Open Sourcing include the following:

- access to code
- no lock in
- no discrimination
- liquid collaboration

Of course, using Open Source code doesn't mean that it will be perfect.

Open Source is expensive

We need companies to sell Open Source code. (point to many examples where this happens today (ELK, ...)

Open Source software is not free. Any code has a cost and a side effect. Using Open Source code doesn't mean that you don't pay for it. It means that you pay in a different way than a direct financial transaction.

Open Source *lingua franca*

It is very important that Open Source and Creative Commons are the *lingua franca* between all players. The take-up of Open Source will help us to remove the 'proprietary lock' of closed software, which creates perverse incentives and does not allow the peripheral countries (or players) to have a strong role in the quality and security of that code. Open Source and Creative Commons allow the best teams and ideas to win, and they reward good behavior. A good system is one where 'less ethical or benign' actors behave well, even when it is against their natural instincts or values.

Closeness and a lack of sharing are more valuable to the attacker than to the defender.

We have a lot of evidence that demonstrates that the more we know about security and risk, the better we can protect and mitigate. It all comes down to how well we communicate, with both tests and TDD.

OpenSource.pt

To increase transparency, the government should ensure the following policies are adopted:

- all code written and paid for by Government agencies to be released under an Open Source license (by 2020)

- all Government-created documents to be released under Creative Commons
- all Portuguese companies to publish their code under Open Source license, and technical documentation under Creative Commons
- pay for Open Source software (in license and per usage)

The financial model that would allow implementation of these ideas needs careful consideration. The key is that the developers of whatever Open Source code is used, should have a revenue stream equivalent to that use, so that they can spend more time working on that software, and hire more developers to work on it.

The government needs to trust their citizens and treat them with respect. This will empower the people, and create economic models that reward them. Don't worry about the big companies, they have enough talent and skills to make money from this model and ideas. In most cases, they are the senior players at the table, and clever companies will adopt this model and thrive on it.

Open the source of Portuguese code

Government and private companies should create venture capital funds to buy existing software companies and Open Source their code. These companies should use part of that money to transform their business model into one based on the Open Source stack. As they wrote it, so they would have a huge competitive advantage. However, local companies would also be able to provide these services.

The return on investment to the Portuguese economy would be much greater than the amount invested.

The next level App Security Social Graph

My core belief is that openness and visibility will eventually create a model/environment where the *'right thing'* tends to happen, since it is not sustainable (or acceptable) to do the *'wrong thing'* (which, without visibility is usually not exposed or contested). See the first couple of minutes of the Git and Democracy presentation[14] for a powerful example of this *'popular/viral awareness'* in action.

When I look at my country (Portugal, and now the UK), or my industry (WebAppSec), I see countless examples of scenarios where, if information was disclosed and presented in a consumable way, much of what happens would not be tolerated.

For example, we in the WebAppSec industry know that bad software and applications are created every day. Both we, and the customers, have accepted that vulnerabilities are part of creating software, and that the best we can do is to improve the SDL, and reduce risk.

If the real scale of the problem was known, would we, either as a society, or an industry, accept it? Would we accept that large parts of our society are built on applications whose workings very few people understand?

The tech world is trying to find ways to connect data sets that makes *'reality understandable/visible'*, so that what is really going on is exposed in a way that is both easy to consume, and actionable.

For example, look at the Next Level Doctor Social Graph[15] for an attempt to drive change in a commercially viable way (See their '"Open Source Eventually"[16] idea)

From that page, here is their description of the problem:

"It is very difficult to fairly evaluate the quality of doctors in this country. Our State Medical Boards only go after the most outrageous doctors. The doctor review websites are generally popularity contests. Doctors with a good bedside manner do well. Doctors without strong social skills can do poorly, even if they are good doctors. It is

---

[14]http://diniscruz.blogspot.co.uk/2012/10/a-must-watch-ted-talk-about-git-and.html

[15]http://www.medstartr.com/projects/82-next-level-doctor-social-graph

[16]http://www.medstartr.com/projects/82-next-level-doctor-social-graph

difficult to evaluate doctors fairly. Using this data set, it should be possible to build software that evaluates doctors by viewing referrals as "votes" for each other." (see related reddit thread here[17])

This is what they call the *Next Level Doctor Social Graph* , and when I read it I thought of doing the same for software/apps under the title: **The next level App Security Social Graph**

Here is the same text with some minor changes (in bold) on what the **The next level App Security Social Graph** could be:

*"It is very difficult to fairly evaluate the quality of **software/application security** in this country. Our **regulators** only go after the most outrageous **incidents/data-breaches**. The **product/services** websites are generally popularity contests. **Applications** with good **marketing do** well. **Applications** without strong **presentation** skills can do poorly, even if they are **secure applications**. It is difficult to evaluate **security** fairly. Using this data set, it should be possible to build software that evaluates **application security** by viewing ..... (to be defined)"*

It would be great if the current debate was on what is ..... *(to be defined)* , ideally with several active experiments figuring out the best metrics, but we are still a long way from that stage of development.

Meanwhile, another **8763** vulnerabilities (change this value to a quantity you think is right) have just been created since you started reading this. These 'freshly baked' vulnerabilities are now in some code repository and will be coming soon to an app that you use. Your best defence is to hope that you are not caught by its side-effects.

---

[17]http://www.reddit.com/r/programming/comments/12aocr/doing_hacktivism_right_i_am_crowdfunding_the/

The cathedral's eyeballs

In the cathedral and the bazaar[18] presentation and book, Eric S. Raymond proposes the Linus law *"given enough eyeballs, all bugs are shallow"* , which is usually also applied to Security.

The problem is that we need those eyeballs.

This could be Portugal's contribution to the world: 'AppSec eyeballs' and 'fix Open Source Software'.

It is imperative that a company or country has core contributors (i.e. strong relationships) with strategic Open Source projects. This is not only essential to retain talent, it should also be done from self-interest.

Principle of Public Access in Sweden

https://en.wikipedia.org/wiki/Freedom_of_information_laws_by_-country#Sweden

"The Principle of Public Access means that the general public is guaranteed insight into activities pursued by government agencies. All official documents handled by government agencies are public unless they contain information specified as secret under the Public Access to Information and Secrecy Act. Each request to take part of official documents is handled individually and classifying documents or information as secret is subject to appeal. The constitution also grants the right for government employees to pass on information without risk of criminal charges or repercussions and the right to attend court proceedings and meetings of legislative assemblies like the Riksdag."

---

[18]https://en.wikipedia.org/wiki/The_Cathedral_and_the_Bazaar

Privacy

Defend privacy

The right to privacy is a human right.

Everyone should be innocent until proven guilty.

The US and the NSA redefined the notion of surveillance to be 'looking at data', rather than 'capturing data'.

Large tech companies' business models are often based on their users having no, or reduced, privacy.

Governments are actively making the internet less secure in order to continue to easily access users' data.

Cryptography

Privacy is a human right and essential for human dignity. Cryptography is a public service and capability, as it enables the end-user to control their data. It is crucial to protect user data. Cryptography also has an excellent tradition of not relying on security by obscurity, or expecting the attacker to have all the code and encrypted data (the only private data are the encryption keys). Strong cryptography is a good thing, especially if it enables the end-user to control their data.

We need a healthy level of civil disobedience in society, or new ideas will not get the space to flourish and gain wider acceptance by society.

Our parents fought against racism, and for pensions, human rights, and rock & roll. It is our turn to realign society and shift the balance of power. This is about removing control from central organizations (governments, big companies) and give them to individuals and collaborative commons. Currently power is in the hands of who controls the networks.

The Need for Disclosure

We need disclosure of what is going on with technology in companies. Companies today, even Open Source ones, don't have to offer full disclosure. The market doesn't work reward good, ethical players. To change this system, we need to use the power of markets to make Government and companies play fairly and correctly. The government could use its purchasing power to define the rules of engagement, and if the EU doesn't like it, then Portugal could sue the EU. It's time we pushed some of our rules and ideas onto the table.

We need to use the new software workflows of DevOps and release-often-feedback loops in wider society.

Whistleblowers have an important role

Whistleblowers are important because they can make the markets more efficient. Whistleblowers are not needed when public actions, and statements, match (the real) private actions.

Of course, there will still be secrets, but in smaller numbers, and they will be very well protected, *"When everything is a secret, nothing is a secret"*.

Protected by law

We need strong technological legislation that will prevent companies from playing the game of 'Security by obscurity', and will protect whistleblowers. "It's only when you lose control (by sharing) the code and ideas that others really embrace it (and own it as their own idea)".

A rule of thumb should be that "if the law is broken, or crimes are committed to disclose materials, it is okay if the benefits from disclosure are worth it". It is important that companies and individuals know that they will not get away with it.

Limited privacy for state and companies

We want the opposite of privacy for companies, instead we want maximum visibility and transparency from them. This will be better for all involved, and will allow for much fairer competition and better profits in the long run.

Technology can be used in a positive way to enable this openness. Many companies will not like any shift toward increased transparency, just as they didn't like when annual reports were mandated in the last century.

Learn from the music industry

For an example of how technology can be used in a perverse and negative way, look at what happened with the music industry. They viewed their customers who used new digital and sharing technologies as criminals, and passed draconian laws designed to protect their own interests, rather than innovating and learning to succeed in the new technological world. A decade was lost, at great cost to artists and the public.

Government

Collaborative Commons

Collaborative Commons provide a great vision for the future and how it could work. It provides a model of an organization where citizens and entities collaborate for common goals.

"...Commons is a third model that breaks with the binomial market-state notion, formed -allegedly- by the only two organizational models able to meet the needs of the population. Although it is not new, new technologies have greatly promoted its expansion and thus the emergence of an economy of collaborative commons (Procomuns, [online], available: http://procomuns.net/wp-content/uploads/2016/03/CommonsDeclarationPolicies_eng_v01.odt.pdf)

Collaborative Commons is greatly empowered by the move towards a **Zero Marginal Cost** society.

- http://commonstransition.org/commons-collaborative-economy-explodes-barcelona/
- http://wiki.commonstransition.org/wiki/Procomuns_statement_-and_policies_for_Commons_Collaborative_Economies_at_European_level
- http://bigthink.com/think-tank/the-collaborative-commons-economy

Government's role

The Government has a big role to play in this transformation, not as a 'Command and Control' entity, but as a benign influence to level the playing field.

A major problem now is that many world governments view technology as a way to exert more control over their citizens.

Code is Law

Software is made of code. Code is law and grows in importance all the time. Code controls Portugal, and so software controls Portugal. The problem is, Portugal controls very little of the software it uses. It is time for Portugal to take control of the software. This should be a strategic objective of both Portuguese companies and the Portuguese government.

Who controls the world?

The world is dominated by entities and companies who control the following areas:

- finance
- technology
- networks (made of technology)
- intellectual property

Unfortunately for Portugal, its strength does not lie in these areas, so Portugal must challenge the rules of the game, and work to align them with its strategy, and sovereign interests, if it wants to become a player.

Moving to Open Source values and activities, and embracing secure coding and hacking will change how this game is played.

Governments can make a difference

Some people have said to me, "If your ideas depend on the Portuguese Government taking action, you should give up now!" This is the wrong attitude. Governments exist to serve their citizens, and as a citizen with ideas for my Government, I have a duty to share them. We, as a tech community, should request the Government to adopt ideas like those discussed here, especially when the benefits are not for a small group of companies, but for a large section of the tech and IT user population.

Iterate exponentially

All ideas presented should NOT be implemented as a Big Policy or a Big Vision! Anyone who tries to sell you a big, expensive solution, that only major companies can implement, is selling a scam. The small changes, and the marginal gains, are the right way to implement DevOps and government policies (see http://m.bbc.co.uk/sport/olympics/19174302).

Iterate exponentially along the following lines:

1. start small
2. deploy
3. learn from deployment
4. make changes
5. return to step 2, and repeat

These are the solutions for SMEs, individuals, and small teams who work on the ground, understand reality, and are accountable to their local communities.

Ministry of Code

Everything is code, including all DevOps scripts and even things like Firewall rules. These should be managed at a high level within Government, in a type of "Ministry of Code".

This ministry should appoint a CTO and CISO for Portugal, and should implement the following proposals:

- create a **Code for Portugal** initiative using a collaborative commons model, similar to the USA's @codeforamerica.
- manage the PHS (Portuguese Hacking Service)
- manage bug-bounty and hacking championships
- commit to only buy, commission, and use applications and websites that
    - release their code under Open Source licenses
    - release their data and schemas under non-restrictive Creative Commons licenses

Clear Software Act

A Clear Software Act, like the 'Clean Air Act', but focused on code quality and security, would go some way to changing the game and how it is played.

Large numbers of our community are resistant to any kind of regulation, and there are many companies that profit from this resistance.

As Upton Sinclair said, "It is difficult to get a man to understand something, when his salary depends upon his not understanding it". The problem however is not regulation and standards, but *bad* regulation and standards. Good regulation, in areas like health and environment, has made major improvements, and we need to do the same for software and code.

Software Testing Institute

We need to measure and visualize the side effects of code, and we need to measure the 'pollution' created by insecure code and apps. We need a focus on quality and services, where we want to encourage innovation and make it easy and cheap to create secure code in Portugal. Portugal could adopt, and use testing to leapfrog more advanced nations.

- http://blog.diniscruz.com/2016/03/when-talking-about-application-security.html

A Software Testing Institute would allow us to measure and capture this information. The work of such an institute should focus on testing code and apps and creating labels for them.

ASAE for code

ASAE (Autoridade de Segurança Alimentar e Económica) Authority for Economic and Food Security

See Software Facts[19]

When regulation loses the plot

We need to learn from what worked and what didn't work with ASAE. There was a chronic lack of common sense and the ASAE seemed to embrace everything negative that is associated with "security regulation".

An ASAE for code mustn't kill innovation and become a 'TAX'. It needs to empower and reward good behavior, and have a common-sense approach to its operations.

As cyber security gets worse, if we don't have good, positive alternatives, an ASAE is exactly what we will get. This is not a good prospect.

Portugal-wide bug bounty

A Portuguese Software Testing Institute could also include bug-bounties as a core activity. Today, there are bug bounties everywhere, and they are a sign of good InfoAppSec. Even the Pentagon

---

[19]http://www.slideshare.net/DinisCruz/2010-11-owaspsoftwarelabels

has a bug-bounty program, and recently announced a further "Hack the Pentagon" bug-bounty initiative[20]. Where are the Portuguese bug-bounties? They should be a core activity of both business and government, and they should receive appropriate investment. Crowdsourcing solutions could also be used. Portuguese bug-bounties would sit perfectly in our Software Testing Institute.

These institutions will lead the creation of standards and metrics for the insurance industry.

Insurance

The insurance industry is key to making this work. It will push for good metrics to measure secure coding and secure deployments (i.e. how code/apps/software are used in the real world). It will provide a way to compare companies and technologies, and this will make the market more efficient.

Many companies will decide to insure insecure code, and teams that create insecure code/apps. That is fine, as long as that information is disclosed. The insurance companies will increase premiums to pay via higher fines and financial losses. The benefit of this approach will be the reduction of risk. Of course, if we get it wrong, we will have quite a mess to deal with.

Of course, Portuguese companies should be leaders in Software Insurance.

Solution is not to buy 'security'

Most Security vendors have inadequate security, and they sell insecure apps, which can have a negative security impact on the purchasing company's entire ecosystem. The solution is to push Open Source code with a secure ecosystem around it.

---

[20]http://www.defense.gov/News/Article/Article/981160/dod-announces-hack-the-pentagon-follow-up-initiative

Code Nationalization

Nationalizing code is a nuclear option for cases where companies refuse to share their code. It is essential to move to a world where good regulation will allow every line of code that is running and touches our data to be

- public
- peer-reviewable by independent parties
- compile-able by independent parties
- signed

This not only includes websites and 'traditional software', but also operating systems, device drivers, IoT devices, network devices, microchips, etc.: in short, anything that can access or manipulate data.

The market, through the power of big customers, can make a difference by 'nudging' code to be Open Sourced.

The Portuguese government should, at the very least, consider the following policies: * Adopt Git for all official documentation * Teach users (i.e. government employees) the paradigm of version control * Develop a Portuguese version of Docker and Git Where is the Portuguese Raspberry PI (which has sold more than 10 million[21])?

European Union

I am a strong European and I believe in Europe. But Europe needs to change, and refocus on country sustainability.

Portugal should not have to 'beg' the EU for funds to support these ideas.

---

[21]http://www.bbc.co.uk/news/technology-37305200

The EU, and other global organizations and companies, should choose to invest in Portugal because they want to benefit from the perfect storm of talent, energy, regulation, focus and activities that will exist here.

They should invest and participate here because it is in their best interests, and it is where they will get the best return on investment. They shouldn't benefit because of some back-room deal that gave them a special tax break or some other financial inducement, which is a kind of soft corruption. The only benefits they should get are the benefits that are available to any company based in Portugal:

- talent (people, students)
- infrastructure (networks, roads, data centers)
- logistics (the Portuguese version of Amazon, provided as a service to the country)

This kind of collaboration and investment is what the EU should be all about:

- a Collaborative Commons
- a global village
- shared care and respect for each other (and their contributions)
- wisdom of the crowd

New currencies for Southern Europe

A good solution for the Euro problem, for weaker economies like Portugal's at least, is to create alternative currencies. We know how to do this now, with blockchain technology. Multiple FinTech companies are exploring all kinds of business models and workflows.

These alternative currencies should be 100% compatible with the Euro, so they can work side-by-side. They could be created by the next generation of Portuguese hackers, who would also enjoy the challenge of hacking a currency.

Investment in infrastructure

One of the roles of government is to invest in infrastructure. In the 21st century, digital logistics are the new roads. We need a model where the Portuguese producer (be they craftspeople or winemakers, olive oil producers, shoemakers, or butchers) is not required to create the infrastructure to sell those products abroad. All these producers should be able to supply the products to a local Portuguese contact, who is in turn connected to a distribution network, that can finally deliver to the consumer.

Design companies

If the producer does not have a good design for their product, there should be a network of design companies to take on this job, with agreed rules of engagement and price scales. The payment for such design work (such as for oranges from the Algarve) should be seen as an investment and not a cost. That investment is a direct injection of money into the Portuguese economy, through the design company or individual who did the job, the company that organized the workflow, and the producer who sold more products.

They could use the Upwork model to distribute this work.

This system needs to be as simple as those of Uber and Amazon.

The Elon Musk model for producing high-value cars needs to be applied to high-value Portuguese products, such as wine. The focus must be on Portuguese emigrants, and their close networks abroad.

Example scenario

Here is an example of this workflow in action.

Two friends are having dinner together.

- Friend A: "This wine is amazing, what is it?"

- Friend B: "It is XYZ, from this local producer in ABC village, you should get some."
- Friend A: "Great idea". He/she then grabs their phone, goes to the 'Buy.pt' app, takes a screenshot of the wine bottle (which is recognized by the App), chooses the quantity to buy, checks the price and delivery date, and, finally, clicks the 'Buy' button
- Friend B: "Did it work?"
- Friend A: "Yes, a very smooth process, it will be delivered to my house (in a different country) in 3 days."
- Behind the scenes (after the Buy button is pressed)
  - Purchase order is sent to the wine maker
  - Next day the winemaker packages the wine (printing the label from an app), and scans the label to indicate that it is ready to be picked up
  - A local transportation company (or individual) gets a job (via an Uber-style workflow) and collects the package
  - The package is delivered to the Hop of the transportation chain (this would be another local transportation company or an individual)
  - That transportation entity (eventually) delivers the package to the next Hop
  - Many hops later (5, 10, 20) the package arrives at the house of the buyer ('Friend A')

Similar Per-to-per transportation workflow already exists in the UK and other countries. Every entity in the delivery chain (each hop), receives a payment for their journey, based on the time and distance they travel, the ability to deliver faster, the size of the package, etc.

In many cases the drivers would already be going to the delivery location, so it would be (just about) pure profit for them.

It is possible to gamify this process, by providing a scorecard to the more active drivers and sellers. Drivers should be aware that the goods they transport help the local and national economy; this work could appeal to their national pride.

The process should also be as personal and as human as possible, using the names of the producers, drivers, clients, countries, and hops travelled.

Of course, this process could also sell products to buyers inside Portugal, and Portugal might be a good place to start the project. However, external customers (from UK, France, Germany, USA, China) will have more purchasing power, and they don't have a local supermarket where they can buy similar Portuguese goods.

Internet-based model

This model is based on how the internet works and how packages are sent from A to B.

On peer-to-peer delivery hops/nodes, the timing of delivery is less important than knowing that 'eventually it gets there'. It is acceptable to lose a couple of packages along the way, as they will be resent through the delivery chain. Central entities (aka routers) manage the flow between nodes/hops.

This system should be used to figure out how to apply social safety nets (pension, overtime, holidays, sick leave, maternity leave) to this, more fluid, type of work practice.

This kind of system needs some Government funding. It qualifies as government investment, as it generates more sales for Portuguese manufacturers and it creates local jobs.

Data should demonstrate that for every euro invested in this distribution network, x euros are created in the Portuguese economy. Since some percentage of those x euros will be paid in taxes, which ideally will be higher than the original investment. There will be some cases where Government will need to artificially create (or pay) for transportation between two hops that lack local players, or, for example, between long distances that can only be covered by train or plane.

Exponential growth

This is a system that must grow organically and exponentially, until it reaches critical mass. In the beginning, it will be very inefficient and expensive, which is why it requires government support. But by using expensive products, the idea is that the cost of the whole service will be enough to cover the cost of the original product and transportation.

Eventually, as more products flow between hops/nodes, it will be possible to optimize them and reduce transportation costs. In such cases the extra money should go to the producer.

Given the fact that with normal supply chains the producer only gets a small percentage of the final sale price, it would be very interesting if the sales performed though this per-to-per channel would generate a higher price for the producer.

An interesting variation would be to apply the Leanpub model, where the buyer can see how much the producer is getting from the purchase price, and can choose to pay more for the product. Leanpub can demonstrate that this model works.

We must find ways to create connections between buyers and sellers, in a similar way to the Kickstarter model.

Open Source the project

All steps should be tracked in real time using mobile apps. All software and data created for this system should be released under an Open Source and Creative Commons license.
Any patents generated by the development of this initiative should be released openly, as Elon Musk did for Tesla[22].

---

[22]https://www.tesla.com/blog/all-our-patent-are-belong-you

Transportation investment fund

For the locations where there is a recurring transportation gap, an investment fund should be created, which would:

1. create a local company using local entrepreneurs (based on car, truck, train, cycle, air transportation modes)
2. make it work locally (capturing workflows to be used by the next generation of these companies)
3. make it profitable (using the flow of packages delivered)
4. spin it off as an independent company (with 15% shares owned by the investment fund and 85% owned by the employees)
5. when that 15% is sold, use that money to top up the investment fund

This fund could be topped up by philanthropic contributions, crowd-funding initiatives, and normal investors. In cases where the 15% of sales generates a good profit, the investment fund would benefit.

Economics

Software can be the source of further inequality in our society, or it can provide a solution to close the pay gaps. Software can control, or provide freedom and liberty. It can erase the rest of our privacy, or it can enhance it and protect our right to privacy. How it behaves depends on who uses it and to what purpose.

Uber

Why should companies like Uber take 20% of a cab fare for a journey taken in Lisbon, when that 20% is removed from the Portuguese economy?

I like Uber, and I often use it, but we must understand its wider implications to society. We need to help existing industry/workers to modernize and compete with new Uber-type industries, or they will face the same fate as 'Encyclopedia Britannica'. The new generation of internet companies are not just making things faster or cheaper, such as communications or music; they are introducing new, and very disruptive business models which are changing society. Companies like Uber ignore many hard-won workers' rights.

The solution is not to ban these kinds of companies or business methods; the solution is to out-innovate them and, if necessary, change the rules of the game they play. For example, they could be required to have open data, and they could be forbidden to hold any lock-in on drivers or user-data.

We must always ask, "Who guards the guardians?".

Portuguese Emigrants

We should use software to create distribution networks to send PT Products to PT emigrants

- Oranges from Algarve
- 'Bom Petisco' tuna
- Bolachas Maria

Education

Skills

Coding & IT skills are critical for large number of industries, including the following:

- cars
- research
- medicine
- finance
- marketing

Git is a core skill

Version control is a fundamental skill that needs to be mastered by everybody who creates a document or data, which is just about every IT user. Git is a great step in the right direction, but it is still too difficult to use for normal users, and it is not seen as a strategic skill set. Nonetheless, productivity and collaboration increase when Version Control is used effectively.

Education

Businesses should work with Universities to teach the following skills:

- app and network testing (unit, integration, end-to-end)
- how to hack into networks and applications (using vulner-able-by-design apps and companies/countries with public bug-bounties)
- modern languages and frameworks (coding in at least ten languages is an excellent advantage to have)

University course

Here is an idea for a three-year curriculum at third level.

- year 1 - Hacking & learn new coding languages
- year 2 - Testing and TDD
- year 3 - Fixing code and DevOps

Students of this course should receive cloud accounts and learn to use state-of-the-art software and services (GitHub, JIRA, Travis, Jenkins, SAST, VisualStudio, IntelliJ, Eclipse, etc.)

Threat Models as strategic activity

Universities should also teach threat modeling, to create professionals who are proficient in threat modeling when they take up employment. Threat modeling professionals must know how to code, and they must have software development (and DevOps) knowledge and experience.

The benefits of this skill are numerous, both to the student or professional who possess the skill, and to industry. Threat modeling can drive change, and it can map out how things work, as it provides a 'single source of truth'. This is not a theoretical activity.

The Portuguese Government, and companies, should be leaders in threat modeling.

CV

The CV as a document is dead (at least for technology); what matters is your public digital footprint in

- GitHub repo
- StackOverflow score
- Quality of Twitter feed
- Personal blog contents

For the developers

If you are developing code today, you should be thinking along the following lines:

- CI automation
- everything is code (including CI scripts, firewall rules, apps authentication models)
- graphs
- containers (aka Docker)
- version control for data storage (aka Git)
- AI and machine learning
- cloud (aka AWS, Azure, Rackspace)
- serverless code (aka AWS lambda)
- liquid code, message queues, self-defending applications, big data etc.

If you are not thinking in this way, you are already legacy (in terms of code), because all these represent the future of code.

Real time unit test execution and Code Coverage

If you code in JavaScript and are not using Wallaby JS, you are living in the Dark Ages, and you will not be able to code in TDD.

Sharing is a Very Emotional and Dangerous Practice

As someone who likes to share a lot of information, I have a very personal experience of what it feels like when you share data, especially in environments that don't promote, or reward, the sharing of information, be it a screen shot, a document, or an idea.

Many companies don't promote sharing, and as a result knowledge doesn't get transmitted. This is a highly inefficient way to work.

When I publish something online, I usually use a kind of 'shitometer' scale to measure reaction to my post. The scale ranges from a couple of hours, to a day, to a week. If there is no allergic reaction to what I've published within three hours, that means my content can't be that bad.

If no one complains within the first 24 hours, it means that the other side has lost the moral authority to complain, and after a week without complaints I consider the cat to be out of the bag. Anyone who objects after a week can't argue that I shouldn't have shared, because they had enough time to complain, but they didn't.

My problem is, why is sharing even a problem? Ideally, you should be able to share without thinking. When you think about the possible consequences of sharing, you may consider the possibility of not being rewarded for sharing. You are more likely to be rewarded for maintaining the status quo.

This can be quite difficult, because by sharing certain information, you can jeopardize a friendship or a business relationship. Nobody wants to alienate a company or a business partner. You may have more important things to worry about in your life, or in your work, than fighting that particular fight.

I believe that one of the jobs of management is not only to promote sharing, and reward the people that share, but also to share themselves. I always find that when I am in a team the more I share, the more other members share because they think, "Well, if that guy can get away with sharing that information, then I can get away with sharing too". My sharing gives cover to others, and it creates a positive cycle as sharing creates more sharing.

Of course, you can also have a negative cycle where nobody shares, or if somebody shares something and gets punished for it, nobody will ever share anything again.

Ultimately, what we want is a situation where the sharing of information is promoted, so we can all learn from each other. The lack of agenda is one of the main advantages of the open model. In an open and creative world, you know things can be shared, and there is already an implicit license to share.

A license gives you the ability to do something, so you don't have to ask permission and that has a profound effect. That is why collaboration happens a lot more even within a company when you have open licenses.

Creating a sharing culture by embracing Creative Commons

Sharing is difficult, but I believe that Portugal, and other countries, should adopt an open-source culture. They should adopt Creative Commons as a core, strategic value that promotes sharing, and sets an agenda where the default approach is to share and collaborate. If you don't share, the quality of your work will be adversely effected.

A culture of sharing should permeate both business and government. However, a reluctance to share important information is the cultural norm, both in Portugal and elsewhere. The idea that if I know, or learn, something valuable, I keep that information to myself so I am the only person who will benefit from it. Even if I am not secretive by nature, but my community does not embrace sharing, then it is very challenging to overcome this attitude and change the culture.

But the culture should change, to one that embraces collaboration and sharing knowledge. In a way, it is an anti-patent concept. In fact, Portugal could invest in, and then game, the patent system, by obtaining and releasing patents to promote the sharing of information, rather than locking the ideas away.

Both governments and business can decide to adopt a more collaborative, sharing approach. In fact, I would argue that the point of government is to share information and knowledge for the greater good of society. For myself, I am working on a solution for sharing my work, regardless of whether others follow suit. If you want to take the lead, or if you want to see who leads the sharing culture at the moment, look at Tesla.

Elon Musk is an amazing individual. When he reached the peak of success, instead of locking his research away as other companies do, he open-sourced, and continues to open-source, a huge number of patents from space exploration, car research, and battery research. This has a levelling effect, and it improves the quality of what everybody else is doing. It also encourages, if not compels, other companies to follow suit, because they start to look bad if they don't open-source and they will have difficulty hiring talent if they don't take a similar approach.

If you can create this amazing ecosystem where people share and collaborate, productivity levels will go through the roof. In short, a culture of sharing and open-sourcing should be a strategic decision because it benefits everyone.

Actions and recommendations

Here is a summary of all the actions and recommendations mentioned and discussed in this book.

Actions

- Develop Open Source code in Portugal by implementing the following policies:
- Release all code written and paid for by Government agencies under an Open Source license (by 2020)
- Release all Government-created documents under Creative Commons
- All Portuguese companies to publish their code under Open Source license, and publish technical documentation under Creative Commons
- Create Portuguese clones of successful apps, services, and products (all based on Open Source technology)
- Hire devs/companies to work on FOSS projects (add ref to 'Open Source is not Free' chapter in book)
- Legalize hacking (of everything inside the Portuguese network)
- Demand secure code, apps, and networks
- Create a 'software commons'
- Take lead in privacy and encryption
- Compel companies ToS that relate to security and privacy to have a maximum of 1024 chars

Recommendations

- Create a venture capital fund to buy existing Portuguese software companies and Open Source their code

- Create a 'Ministry of Code', a 'Junior Minister of DevOps', and national-level positions of CTO and CISO (like the US has)
- Copy US initiative Code for America (@codeforamerica), using a collaborative commons model
- Allocate 10% of the current military budget to fund investment in cyber/app security, digital infrastructure, and the huge skills shortage in these areas
- Introduce strong technological legislation that will prevent companies from playing the game of 'security by obscurity', and will protect whistleblowers
- Commit, with participating companies, to only buy, commission and use applications/websites that
    - a) have released their code under Open Source licenses
    - b) have released all their info and schemas under non-restrictive Creative Commons licenses
- Adopt Git for all official documentation
- Teach users (i.e. government employees) the paradigm of version control
- Develop a Portuguese version of Docker and Git
- Attract Tesla to build factories and R&D facilities in Portugal

Other recommendations

- Export to CPLP, Europe and the world, thousands of cyber/AppSec specialists who will be??/ have been trained in Portugal
- Create technical content in Portuguese
- Digital identities and e-Residency solution, just like Estonia

Recommendations for education and training:

Businesses should work with Universities to teach the following skills:

- App and Network Testing (unit, integration, end-to-end)
- How to hack into networks and applications (using vulnerable-by-design apps and companies/countries with public bug-bounties)
- Modern Languages and Frameworks (coding in at least ten languages is an excellent advantage to have)
- Threat modelling

Teach everyone to hack:

- Introduce 'Hacking Service' where everyone needs to learn how to code and use technology (like the old Portuguese military service)
- Organize and host regular Hackathons and bug-bounty championships, as part of a new, national, hackathon league.
- Train cyber/AppSec specialists using similar techniques to the ones we use to train doctors, nurses, and other medical professionals

Why Portugal?

Easier in a small country

It is easier to implement these ideas in a smaller country, which is more likely to have fewer agendas and fewer lobby groups wielding influence. We already have the power to make these changes. Being able to make them is an important aspect of Portugal's sovereignty and independence.

Of course, you can replace Portugal with any other country in the world, especially any European country. But I am Portuguese, so I have a soft spot for Portugal, and I know that Portugal has exceptional talent, exceptional AppSec people who could make this happen. What we need is focus and determination.

The following aspects of Portuguese life, culture, history, education, and economic environment make it an ideal location to implement these ideas:

- good pool of InfoSec and AppSec talent
- a supply of engineers
- strong sense of ethics and community
- good engineering and math education
- good problem solving ability

Portugal has hit rock-bottom with multiple financial crises and a European bailout. The only way is up. Portugal has learned the hard way what it feels like to be the junior player (i.e. The financial markets' speculation on Portugal's economy helped to create the situation that lead to the EU bailouts).

Raise the bar of the discussion

We live in an era where ideas are not debated, experts are ignored, science is not respected, and lies are accepted. This is very dangerous for us, for our children and for Portugal. Eleanor Roosevelt[23] is credited with saying "Great minds discuss ideas; average minds discuss events; small minds discuss people". I want to discuss and act on ideas, not events or people. We need a better, more informed, more knowledgeable, and more empowered media, to keep the system accountable.

Big questions

We are currently faced with big questions and changes on privacy, liberty, humanity, freedom, work, all of which are centred on technology and secure code, and these questions need to be discussed, understood and addressed. There are no perfect solutions.

We need to achieve a workable compromise and make sure we take the best course of action.

I don't claim that all my ideas are good, that they will work or are even all realistic, especially in the current political and economic ecosystem, but I know that big changes occur when we head in the right direction and can experiment, adapt, refactor and improve.

Best in 'graduating high school'?

What is Portugal best at[24] is a world map that shows what every country leads the world in (2014).

According to this map, Portugal has the best rate for 'graduating high school'. We can do better than that. We should be world leaders in software, craftsmanship, cyber security, secure coding, DevOps, and food, and we should expand the market of those products. Portugal should not compete on cheap labor, but on the following resources:

---

[23]http://quoteinvestigator.com/2014/11/18/great-minds

[24]http://www.businessinsider.com/what-countries-are-best-at-2014-1?IR=T

- advanced technology
- people
- skills
- infrastructure
- ability to deliver

Not the 'sweat-house', but the 'power-house'.

Protect the internet

The internet is one of the biggest gifts given to humanity. Its founders made it open and free (in terms of both cost and freedom). The success of the internet is a testament to those decisions and their values.

Now, the time has come for our generation to continue in their footsteps and keep the internet open and free for the next generation. It is our turn to realign society and shift the balance of power. This is about removing control from central organizations (governments, big companies) and giving control to individuals and collaborative commons.

Portugal needs to export engineers

Everyone who leaves Portugal brings Portugal with them. They become an ambassador for Portugal, and they become a consumer of Portuguese products (assuming they are easy to buy from abroad). Many of them have connections with Portuguese companies, and could bring jobs back to Portugal in the future. Everyone who leaves Portugal will learn new skills, and eventually return with those skills, experience, and references, which are, of course, a net gain for Portugal.

Portugal and Europe need diversity and indigenous activities and industry, to ensure their futures. In Europe, sometimes it seems that we have forgotten "Why XYZ was done and what was its objective".

The next generation of manufacturing is going to be local (to a country, city, company, even a house). This is the Age of Sustainability. Portugal needs to be technologically independent and sustainable.

Amazon is a great model for Portugal (Shopping, AWS, logistics). How many senior and experienced Amazon ex-employees work in Portuguese Government and technology initiatives?

What is the future of Portugal?

Is it to be a garden for Europe, a holiday destination? A small pawn in the global forces that control the world?

Or could Portugal work together with the CPLP (Community of Portuguese Speaking Countries) in a united partnership that provides significant opportunities? Portugal could become a Powerhouse of Technology that inspires and leads the world in secure coding

Sail the Code

Let's use code to create a generation with a strong work ethic and values.

Let's create a new reality for Portugal.

In the same way that Portuguese navigators once looked at the unknown sea and conquered it, our new digital navigators must do the same with code.